BEYOND WINNING

BEYOND WINNING

KESHAVAN NAIR

PARADOX PRESS

Published by Paradox Press
12629 North Tatum Blvd., Suite 161
Phoenix, AZ 85032

Nair, Keshavan 1932
Beyond Winning
1. Leadership
1. Managers and Leaders

87-062803
ISBN 0-945150-19-9
Printed and bound in the United States of America
Printing by George Lithograph Company

To P.N., who will be pleased to see this book in print;
and to Robba, who made it possible.

CONTENTS

●
vii

PREFACE

There is a crisis in the quality of leadership today. Many people believe that government and corporate leaders and managers are motivated primarily by self-interest and short-term success. But our fast-changing interdependent society now, more than ever, needs leaders who are not just short-term "winners" but leaders effective enough to have long-term positive impacts on organizations and people.

Many recent books on management stress immediate results and short-term success. To convince readers of the validity of their methods, they rely heavily on anecdotes and vignettes about currently popular leaders. This approach can be persuasive and makes interesting reading, but it has several drawbacks. Because such books are not intended to be careful historical studies, they rarely tell the full story. Many of the purported "successes" do not stand the test of time. Like high fashion, the examples are interesting for one season only.

I felt there was room for a book that went "forward to basics," stating essential ideas on leadership and management with a brief commentary but not relying on contemporary examples to bolster the arguments. The reader is thus challenged to reflect on the ideas and determine how they apply to his or her immediate situation. Then, as situations change, the reader can come back to the book. *Beyond Winning* is designed for rereading; it is a book to be used, not just read once and stored away.

Several people contributed greatly to the development of the book. The proficiency of Ellen Carr, assisted by Leslie Roberts, on the word processor, as well as their encouragement and cheerful disposition made the rewrites easier. Steve James's insightful comments and Tralelia Twitty's editorial assistance significantly improved the clarity of the text, while Barbara Ziller's design enhanced the visual impact and readability of the book. David Canaan's subtle suggestions had a significant positive impact. Jim Beley of Fog Press typeset the book, using the latest in electronic publishing techniques. I am grateful for the support of these individuals.

Robba Benjamin reviewed the entire manuscript. Without her criticism, encouragement, and leadership example, the book could not have been completed.

●
x

INTRODUCTION

The invention and mastery of labor-saving machines—the challenge of the industrial age—is largely behind us, and we have met that challenge brilliantly. Technology has enabled us to fly higher, to respond faster, to produce vast quantities of goods at lower prices than ever before. However, somewhere along the way, while developing an increasingly sophisticated relationship with machines, we have lost our sense of *people.*

Our single-minded quest to automate, our fixation with attaining mastery over inanimate objects, and our obsession with reducing everything to numbers have produced an overemphasis on management at the expense of leadership. Technology can be managed—and we are very good at that. People, however, have to be led.

The human-machine interface is easier to understand than the interaction between human beings. The management of things is the challenge of the past; the leadership of people is the challenge of the future. Addressing the needs and desires of other human beings within a moral framework forces us to ask questions about ourselves. This type of self-examination is not taught in schools of business and government, and is not compatible with the autocratic leadership that exists in many organizations. In fact, very little in our formal education or experience prepares us to be effective leaders of people.

The leadership techniques developed by industry and the military, which are used by many of our current leaders, are obsolete for leading people in the postindustrial information-based society. These leaders achieved success under conditions that no longer exist, namely, a work force with little education, limited mobility, and severely restricted rights to recourse against their superiors, as well as consumers who had no rights and only limited choices.

In business the emerging, broadly defined global economy is characterized by many competitors worldwide, all of whom have access to equivalent technology, equipment, and raw materials. New production techniques, a key competitive differentiator in the industrial age, are rapidly communicated and copied. The challenge for all companies, then, lies in more effective management of the human element. The sustainable competitive advantage will be the dedicated, innovative, quality- and service-conscious employee. In the postindustrial age we will have to pay attention to the needs of every employee and consumer. This will be the key to superior, consistent financial performance.

National and local governments, whose primary function is service, have committed themselves to technology. They know more about the people they serve than ever before, yet they alienate them. But this alienation cannot be blamed on technology; it is the result of an outmoded style of leadership.

Through practice and repeated success we have become experts at managing an outmoded problem. From the mistakes in Vietnam to the decline in the United States' competitive position, we can see the failure of overemphasis on management by numbers combined with a neglect of the leadership of people. The future requires a new kind of leader, one as concerned about process as outcomes, one as committed to quality as quantity, one as focused on people as on production.

There is no escaping the need for leaders. Leadership impacts every aspect of society. National resolve in domestic and foreign policy, competitiveness in business, responsiveness by local government, preservation of the family unit, even the ascendancy or decline of sports franchises — everything in today's society is affected by the quality of leadership.

Beyond Winning explores the concept of **positive leadership.** It is for those who believe that the time has come to address the changing needs of our society. It is also for those who are beginning to wonder whether the price of "winning at all costs" is not more than we are prepared to pay. The balancing of organizational purpose with justice for the individual is the major challenge of positive leadership.

What, then, distinguishes the positive leader?

- Positive leaders will set objectives for the organization which are of benefit to their constituencies, can be achieved with integrity, and are within the framework of the values of a just and fair society.

- Positive leaders will recognize that all achievements of the organization are a result of actions by people in it. These leaders will always treat the people in the organization as its most valuable asset.

- Positive leaders will motivate people to higher achievement with encouragement and support, not through fear and intimidation.

- Positive leaders will never take credit for the work of others and never fail to take full responsibility for their own mistakes. They do not sacrifice others to make themselves look good.

- Positive leaders will leave behind organizations ready to face the next challenge, with individuals willing and able to take on the role of leadership.

Positive leaders put into practice what many of our current leaders now only preach.

To be effective, a positive leader must **act;** attain **power** in order to act effectively; develop **influence,** because power alone is not sufficient; understand and adapt to **change;** and nurture **paradox** by encouraging a diversity of ideas. How well a leader does these things is founded in the individual's **character.** *Beyond Winning* is organized around these six concepts.

Individuals in leadership positions have power and are usually action-oriented and effective in influencing others, but this does not make them positive leaders. To advance to positive leadership, the first step is to act after thought, exercise power with compassion, and influence with integrity.

The extra dimension required to reach the full level of positive leadership comes from having the ability to understand and adapt to change, the wisdom not just to tolerate but also nurture opposites, and the character and courage to be steadfast and yet admit mistakes.

The climb to positive leadership is beyond the capabilities of many of today's so-called leaders. The required extra dimension runs counter to the excessive egos and driving personal ambition that they have developed over several decades of winning at all costs. If you are convinced that you are a positive leader, you probably are not one. Only the people you are supposed to lead can determine whether you are a positive leader.

There are no "cookbooks" for leadership. In that spirit, *Beyond Winning* presents not instructions but ideas. These ideas are stated simply and briefly. Challenge yourself to see which of the ideas apply to your situation. It is only through such intellectual effort that you will advance the quality of your leadership. Knowledge is obtained not by reading but by reflecting on what you have read—and then putting it into practice.

Leadership is not the gift of genius; it can be learned. You already have some of the necessary qualities — and can acquire the others through hard work, dedication, and commitment to your purpose. Positive leadership is not complicated in concept, but it is very difficult to practice.

Positive leadership does not belong to any one culture or system. It is the heritage of all people. Everybody has the opportunity for leadership at one time or another, whether in business, politics, sports, community activities, or family. Take advantage of these opportunities as they arise. Then go a step further—become a positive leader.

Leadership is a never-ending journey. I hope that this book will help you along the way. Pick up *Beyond Winning* again when you change jobs, when you are promoted, when you face new challenges and take on new responsibilities, when your career is at a standstill—or when you just want to refresh your ideas about leadership.

"It is not sufficient that you be a person of action, you must also be perceived as one. The organization's perception of you as a person of action is essential to your effectiveness as a leader."

1
ACTION

Your actions are the visible manifestations of your leadership. They must move the organization toward its objectives.

Action is making things happen. Decisions are the recipe for action. Implementation translates the recipe into reality. The proof is in the results.

The performance of any organization is the result of actions. To lead, you must become a person of action.

Action is initiated when you perceive a challenge, whether threat or opportunity. Your action will be appropriate only if you can correctly identify the challenge.

Develop clarity about the challenge. This is the critical first step. With clarity, difficult choices will be made easy. There can be no easy choices if there is confusion about the challenges that you face.

When you cannot act, it is because you don't know what your purpose is.

As a positive leader, you will think about your actions in the framework of your value system. Thought is the conscience of action. Action without thought invites disaster.

Never get so busy doing things that you forget to think about what you are doing. From the horrors of the Holocaust to the foolish disasters of Watergate and the Bay of Pigs, people of action had stopped thinking about what they were doing. When people of action become robots, they lose their values. A person of action who has unethical values always leads the organization astray.

Do not define the challenge to fit your idea of the action. Let the problem dictate the solution. Only by doing this will your actions be relevant.

The world is full of solutions looking for problems. This approach may be suitable for academics but not for a person of action. Tackling the right problem is the essence of successful action.

It is not sufficient that you be a person of action, you must also be perceived as one. The organization's perception of you as a person of action is essential to your effectiveness as a leader.

Most people do not see you making decisions on important things. It is decisiveness about small things that influences their opinion of you as a person of action. At meetings of your colleagues, try to be the one who summarizes. In business, every meeting in which you are the senior executive should end with a decision made by you.

At times, inaction is appropriate. One does not clear up muddy water by stirring it. To be effective, your choice of inaction must be perceived as decisive.

Inaction is perceived as action when the choice is deliberate. It takes wisdom to determine when a problem will resolve itself. Intervention usually worsens such situations. Communicating your decision to "leave it alone" is essential. Deliberate "benign neglect" will thus be perceived as decisive.

Your actions need purpose. Purpose is provided by your vision for the organization. Your vision is the destination; your purpose is to get there.

Action without a vision is like shooting without a target — it is aimless. If you know where you are going, you can decide how to get there. If you don't know where you are going, all paths will get you there. Everything you do should be related to getting to your destination. When there is purpose, the energies of the organization, focused like a laser, can cut through any obstacles. When there is no purpose, actions are not bound together and lack the strength to move the organization forward.

9

When you have a vision for the organization, there will be order. You will devote your energies to the important problems, and unimportant problems will not take up your time. When there is no vision, unimportant problems appear important and the important problems are not adequately addressed.

When there is a vision and order, problems are addressed quickly but without haste. Even in a crisis the actions are deliberate and well thought out.

When you have a clear vision for the organization, you will be in control and your attention will be focused on important problems. If you read the history of empires, monarchies, and businesses in their decline you will find one common factor: The people in power were occupied with unimportant problems.

" You must construct your vision with great care. In matters of vision, simplicity is power. You should be able to explain your vision to any individual in your organization. "

You must formulate a vision that is independent of any but the most significant external changes. Vision is the reason for the existence of the organization. It should not be changed often. Consider changing the vision only when there is a significant discontinuity.

Be skeptical of arguments that suggest another destination is more desirable. Every level in the organization is affected by a change in vision. If you change destinations, make sure that you have the means and know the way to get there. If you are a CEO, investment bankers and consultants will place possible acquisitions before you. Commitment to your vision will provide the most effective screening device. Leaders are always being pressured to change and to be responsive to popular opinion. But that is followership, not leadership.

If you become the leader when a change in vision is necessary, consider it an opportunity and a challenge. Making the appropriate change requires insight and courage.

●
11

If your vision (destination) is obviously important and very difficult to achieve, you will have no competition. Your rewards will be great if you succeed; but even in failure, people will admire you. Leadership marries the art of the possible with the challenge of the vision.

There are no traffic jams on the way to the summit of Mt. Everest. Even those who failed are on the honor roll of mountaineers.

Difficulty is a moving frontier. Providing the power of computers to the masses was an obviously important and difficult challenge. The pioneers had little competition, achieved great recognition, and gained large financial rewards. But as the difficulty declined, competition increased and many of the pioneers faltered. You must advance to the next level of difficulty if you are to minimize competition.

You must construct your vision with great care. In matters of vision, simplicity is power. You should be able to explain your vision to any individual in your organization.

Your vision is determined by the way you answer three important questions: What activity are we engaged in? What do we want to achieve? What values will we adhere to in our conduct?

Large groups of people cannot commit themselves to complex ideas. When they are presented with a complex idea, they will simplify it for their use. The problem is that their simplification may be inappropriate.

The words that you choose to express your vision are extremely important in obtaining commitment from the organization. Politicians have always recognized the importance of encapsulating the ideals of their complex programs in simple phrases. American presidents have used names such as New Deal, New Frontier, and Great Society to sell their programs to the public.

●
13

You have to decide where you are going before you decide how you are going to get there.

Objectives and goals are like milestones by which to measure your progress. Strategy is how you are going to achieve your objectives. Do not waste your time on strategic decisions until you have formulated a vision and specified your objectives. If you are not reaching your goals, you need to reevaluate your strategic decisions. Do not modify your milestones to match your progress.

When you think of vision and strategy, do not be confused by the terminology of means and ends. Ends are means, and means can become ends.

You can think of the vision as the end, but the vision for the organization is also the means to motivate the people in the organization. Profits are the means for a business to pay dividends and bonuses and to invest in the business. Profits are also thought of as goals for operating managers. It depends on where you stand. Are rivers the means to fill the ocean, or are oceans the means to create rain and snow to fill the rivers?

•
14

Decisions are the precursors to action. The success of your actions depends on your decision-making skills.

Some decision-making skills can be taught, but theory has its limits. The ability to recite the recipe doesn't mean you can prepare the dish.

Making decisions under pressure has to be learned on the job. You have to get into the water to learn to swim.

Your decisions must address two questions: What should we do and how should we do it? The first deals with effectiveness, the second with efficiency.

What you should do is dominated by your vision and the competitive situation. The major influence on *how* you do something is related to the internal workings of the organization. You need to know how to get things done efficiently.

●
15

❝Right answers are contained in the right questions. ❞

When you are engaged in competition, your decisions are strategic. A fundamental concept of strategy is the consideration of what your competition may do. If you make your choice without that consideration, you are relying on pure skill or chance — not strategy.

In a competitive framework, your organization and your competitors have both common and conflicting objectives. In business, common objectives may exist with respect to the overall well-being of the industry and possible positions on regulatory issues. Conflicting objectives may be present in areas such as market share, new product introductions, and geographic expansion. However, in all cases, strategy selection should consider the options available to your competitors.

If you are a leader, you have common and conflicting objectives with your colleagues. In business, the firm's success is a common objective. But since there can be only one CEO, senior executives are also competing. In politics, all candidates want their party to win the White House, but they compete to be the nominee.

In making decisions you will face the Four Horsemen: Insufficient Information, Uncertainty, Time Constraints, and Competing Objectives. You need tools to fight with, even if you cannot conquer.

The tools you need for making decisions are simplified models of your enterprise. You have developed them through experience, and you know they work. These models do not provide detailed answers; rather, they evaluate answers. They allow you to ask the right questions. Right answers are contained in the right questions.

The objective of modeling is insight, not numbers. The models you use in making decisions must be simple and not too precise. An inflexible model can become a foolish consistency.

You cannot develop simple decision-making models without a deep understanding of the decision-making situation. Understanding comes from analysis, experience, and reflection. Simple models will allow you to make effective decisions rapidly — and you will be perceived as a person of action. Do not search for the perfect model. A good approximation is what you require; otherwise you will develop analytical paralysis.

Because changing conditions are inevitable, a model must be able to respond to them. It must accommodate change just as readily as water adapts to different containers. A precise model can, therefore, be a handicap. Individuals who cannot tolerate the ambiguity of imprecise plans make poor leaders.

All models of reality are incomplete. The ability to recognize incompleteness is a sign of maturity. This is also true of knowledge. No person or group of people can know everything. Admitting ignorance is the beginning of wisdom.

The art of developing a practical and realistic model is in deciding what has to be included and what can be left out. In this sense your models will of necessity be incomplete. Incompleteness implies that there is the potential for error in your evaluations. You must, therefore, keep an open mind when presented with alternative points of view.

Many models have been encapsulated in rules. Every organization has them, even though the reasons for their existence may be long forgotten. These "hand-me-down" models can result in decisions based on custom instead of thought, on opinions rather than facts. ("But we've *always* done it this way.") Do not fall into this trap. Beware of outmoded models. Question their appropriateness to current conditions — you may need to develop your own models. This verification process is your opportunity for gaining a deeper understanding of your circumstances.

Consideration of strategic issues is not enough. You must also evaluate issues of chance in reaching a decision.

Issues of chance are related to events outside the control of those involved in the competitive situation. Consider a general in war. Decisions must take into account what the enemy might do (the strategic aspect) as well as what the weather may be (the chance aspect).

As an executive for a financial institution, you have to decide what rate you should pay on deposits. You have to consider what your competitors might do (strategic issues) and what the interest rate environment will be (chance issues).

●

Good decision-making models are often very simple, but developing them is very difficult.

Without understanding the complex realities of the issues that have to be addressed, it is not possible to develop realistic, simple models. To develop a good approximation, you must know the "correct" solution. Only then can you evaluate the accuracy of your approximation. These simple models are useful only if they are sufficiently accurate for decision-making purposes *and* save time in their application.

In making decisions, include the information provided by analysis and models but be guided by your experience and judgment.

There is more to the art of leadership than technique. Like a good driver, you should strive to develop a feel for the road. It is your integrative and intuitive abilities coupled with your experience that will make you a successful leader. As Napoleon said, "Commanders-in-chief are to be guided by their own experience or genius." However, be skeptical of the appropriateness of your experience and judgment in a new environment. Napoleon's judgment was not infallible in his Russian campaign.

If you have a string of successes, beware of overconfidence. Remember that there was always an element of chance in your success. Skepticism, and even doubt, may lead to long-term success and to the elimination of blunders.

Victors rarely believe in chance. When you are overconfident, you will not listen to competing arguments and your strength of character, which is so essential to making courageous decisions, can become stubbornness. Overconfidence clouds judgment and breeds failure.

You must make things happen to be perceived as a person of action. Because an organization is a web of interdependencies, you always have to negotiate with others to achieve your goals.

You cannot make things happen without the cooperation of others. Negotiation is often not for immediate requirements but in anticipation of future needs. Develop your negotiation skills.

Competition *and* cooperation are at the core of negotiating. It is extremely important that you understand your mixed motives as a negotiator. You compete with your colleagues in attempting to attain some of your objectives, and you cooperate with them in achieving the organization's objectives.

If you are too competitive, your colleagues will not cooperate; if you compromise too readily, your ideas will not be implemented. In either case, you will be ineffective.

Your participation in implementation, even if only symbolic, is essential to your being perceived as a person of action.

Implementation creates results out of decisions. The general who visits the battlefield, the politician who tours the urban renewal project, the CEO who makes the round of the shop floor are all symbolizing their involvement in implementation. To lead, you must inspire; the people who carry out your decisions need to identify with you. To be perceived as a person of action, you have to occasionally be *in* the action.

"The wise exercise of power is the most challenging activity of leadership. Power corrupts subtly. It is the true test of character."

2
POWER

Power is the ability to do what you want to do when you want to do it. We are all both powerful and powerless.

Heads of state and corporate executives command great resources. They are powerful. Nevertheless, events and institutional constraints can dominate them and make them powerless.

Even with the power to command resources, the power to achieve your objectives will be elusive. Both Hitler and Napoleon had the power to command great armies, but the Russian winter was not theirs to control. A CEO has power over the organization, but factors such as exchange rates, regulations, natural disasters, sabotage, and human error cannot be controlled.

Bureaucracies can make leaders powerless. Like an army of ants, they can overthrow the elephant.

Power is a function of dependency. If you are dependent on someone, that person has power over you.

Power implies not doing what you do not want to do. Your ambitions and desires are constraints on your power. People who control what you want (e.g., your promotions and salary) have power over you and can make you do things you do not want to do. The more uncertain you can be made to feel about the outcome, the greater their power. This is why many CEOs wish to maintain a level of unpredictability in their behavior: It is an exercise of power.

Power over oneself is the most difficult power to attain. Power over oneself liberates. Absolute power over oneself liberates absolutely. It is power over others that corrupts. When you have power over yourself, power over others will flow to you.

You will have no need for aggressive or dictatorial behavior if you have power over yourself. Self-mastery enables the effective exercise of power over others. As if by gravity, such power flows naturally toward those with self-mastery.

Chinese philosopher Lao-tzu explained the flow of power in this way: "How did the great rivers and seas get their kingship over the hundred lesser streams? Through the merit of being lower than they; that was how they got their kingship."

There are two types of power in an organization: executive power and implementation power. Executive power controls implementation power.

A person with executive power decides what has to be done, who does it, and when it will be completed. Implementation power is related to controlling the process of getting something done. It is the power associated with the task leader, the operations manager, and the supervisor. To learn to successfully exercise executive power, first become a good implementer, then move on. If you cling to implementation, you will never rise to executive power. If you spend all your time doing things, when will you find time to decide what to do? If you try to bypass the implementation learning experience, your power will sink in the quicksand of bureaucracy.

●
25

In an organization, you start with implementation power. By successfully exercising and delegating it, you rise to executive power. You need to show that you can perform before you can decide what others should do.

You have to pay your dues; this is one of the rites of reaching leadership. The implementation tasks provide the opportunity to show that you can do things, not just think about them. Task leader, supervisor, field operative — these positions are the vehicles with which to demonstrate your leadership and show that you are ready for executive power. You need to have been a lieutenant leading your squad into battle before you can be a general and send others into battle.

You lose control to the extent that you delegate executive power. Delegate executive power sparingly, and then only to competent people loyal to your vision.

There are various levels of executive power. At the highest level, you set the direction of the organization. Within that framework, lower levels of power can be given to the head of each department or functional area. Selecting the right people is the key to the effective delegation of power. As Walter Wriston, former chairman of Citicorp, said, "If you have the right person in the right place, there is almost no way that you can get hurt; if you have the wrong person in that place, there is no way you can save yourself."

You maintain executive power by letting others develop options and prepare decision recommendations, but reserving for yourself the final decision.

"Power over oneself liberates. Absolute power over oneself liberates absolutely. It is power over others that corrupts."

The powerful leader defines the vision and sets the destination for the organization. But responsibility does not end there — one must also monitor progress.

Accurate information on the progress of implementation is essential to the successful exercise of power. The commanding general, the executive, the football coach, all have to continuously monitor the progress toward their objectives.

The Mongol conqueror Genghis Khan established an elaborate system of horseback messengers who brought him information from distant battles and outlying provinces. He valued information so highly that everyone, even the royal princes, had to make way for these messengers and provide horses when necessary. To the same end, business executives have elaborate information systems and political leaders have intelligence agencies.

●
27

The sources of power in an organization are not fixed. Anticipate future power sources correctly and you will have found a key to gaining power.

In national policy, candidates try to be the first to raise new issues. If you are in business, look for the new growth areas and the functions that will provide competitive advantages in the future. Make these issues and areas your own. When they become important, you are likely to be elevated to positions of power.

Think of organizational change as a redistribution of power. It is a time for gaining power.

Business reorganizations may occur because of changes in functional requirements driven by technology, customer requirements, and regulations. These reorganizations are opportunities for gaining power. When a person of power leaves a key position, the distribution of power will change. Institutions attempt to avoid the redistribution of power by endowing the office and not the person with power. Such attempts are only partially successful, since no two prime ministers, presidents, or other leaders are equally powerful.

To be a person of power, you must seek power. You should play by the rules, but you do not have to think by them. For you to gain power, somebody else must lose it. If you are not prepared to accept power from others, you will not be a person of power.

It takes courage to seek power. When others show weakness or lack of courage and become indecisive, you have the opportunity to step into the vacuum and let power flow to you. When there is chaos, the bold leader gains power.

Accepting positions of power entails risk. When you exercise power, you will be held responsible for the outcome. If you have power, there will be others who will seek to take it from you.

Projection of power is essential to the exercise of power. In an organization, those who are perceived to have power will get what they want.

Power is projected through actions and symbols. Both are necessary. Throughout history, those who have exercised power have understood the importance of symbols. The pomp and splendor of monarchs, the trappings of the presidency, the uniforms of generals, and the robes of bishops, cardinals, and popes are important as symbols of power.

When seeking power, do not be deluded by symbols. Accept symbols only *after* acquiring power.

Symbols are useful for projecting power, but they are not a substitute for power itself. Clever individuals will ply you with symbols to satisfy your desire for power. Avoid being "kicked upstairs" with no increase in power.

Leadership confers power. If you are a leader, there are followers. You can set the agenda and they will help you accomplish it. You have power. When the organization considers itself fortunate in having you as its leader, then you have the greatest power.

Your power over an organization depends on how much the organization needs you and how little you need the organization.

If the organization needs you but you have many options, your bargaining ability is great. If the organization needs you but it has many other viable options, then your power is limited.

The wise exercise of power is the most challenging activity of leadership. Power corrupts subtly. It is the true test of character.

That power is the ultimate test of a person's character was well understood by the ancient Greeks. As Sophocles points out in *Antigone,* "No man can be truly known, in heart and hopes and purpose, till the tests of power and government make manifest his nature." Power does not corrupt suddenly. It is like gaining weight — it happens almost imperceptibly. Continued vigilance is necessary to prevent corruption.

You seek power so that you can exercise it. Power is not to be possessed, it is to be used. If you cannot exercise power, you do not have it.

Leadership positions provide the opportunity to exercise power. You have to use the opportunity. It is how you exercise power in your position — not your title — that determines how powerful you are.

The exercise of power will make you powerful. If you do not have the opportunity to exercise power that is commensurate with your ability, then it is time for a change.

Power brings with it moral dilemmas. You must prepare yourself for dealing with these. The fundamental nature of the moral dilemmas does not change with increased power.

Power provides the opportunity for you to exercise a significant amount of control over the lives of others. The moral dilemmas remain the same: the good of the many versus pain for the few, personal values versus corporate policies, national and corporate interests versus individual conscience. Positive leaders look for and address the moral dimension in exercising power.

You, as a leader, must accept the reality that your decisions can affect everyone in the organization. This is a burden of leadership and power.

You can claim some of the credit for success, but you also have to shoulder some of the blame in times of failure. In business, laying off people shows you have failed as a leader. It was your responsibility to have maintained market share, developed new business, and introduced new products. When thousands of workers in Detroit were laid off because of the effects of foreign competition, it was a failure of leadership in the American automobile industry.

●
31

In an organizational context, power gives you the authority to do certain things. It does not confer on you any wisdom. Recognition of this truism is necessary to exercise power successfully over a long time.

Just because people do what you tell them does not mean it is right. One of the problems of power is that it discourages independent thought. Power can be like an addictive drug: It can dull your mind, cloud your judgment, and convince you of your infallibility.

Power is in the quality of the resources you control.

Some people think that having a large number of people reporting to them constitutes power, but they are wrong. It is the abilities of the people who report to you, their willingness to follow your leadership, and what they can accomplish that give you power. The general with superior weapons and a better-trained army is more powerful than one with greater numbers but inferior quality. Choose quality over quantity if you seek to increase power.

You cannot lead by the numbers, though you may be judged by them.

If you lead people effectively, they will take care of the numbers. The organization will produce the results if you provide the leadership. Leaders who rely solely on numbers tend to treat people as statistics. They may have some short-term successes, but they will build nothing of lasting value.

You must lead the people in your organization, but also be one of them. This is the hallmark of a positive leader.

Great leaders know how to rise above the people they lead yet still be one of them. Even though he was revered by them, the people's affection for Gandhi made him one of them.

When you lack the will to exercise power, or you lack the skills because of a change in circumstances, it is time to relinquish power.

When the time comes, give away power with swift strokes. Do not make leeches of those who should succeed you. If you keep power too long you will endanger your achievements. Giving up power to competent successors at the appropriate time is the ultimate test of a wise leader.

●
33

"**C**reate commitment. It is more efficient in influencing people than commanded obedience. Commitment enables individuals to work to their full potential; the obedient do only what is necessary. "

3

INFLUENCE

Power is necessary, but it is not sufficient to get things done. Although authority can force compliance, willingness to comply generates superior performance.

Giving orders is not enough to get things done. Individuals are inspired, not coerced, to superior performance. As a leader, you must inspire commitment, trust, loyalty, and achievement.

You cannot ask people to be loyal to you if you are not loyal to them. Loyalty to the people you lead requires that you act as you wish them to act, never take credit for their work, and never let them take the blame for your mistakes. In every field of activity, commitment by the leadership inspires commitment in the organization.

Create commitment. It is more efficient in influencing people than is commanded obedience. Commitment enables individuals to work to their full potential; the obedient do only what is necessary.

Commitment is created through a vision that people can believe in *and* actions consistent with that vision. Individuals go the extra mile when there is commitment. When people are committed, you can spend your time leading them, not monitoring their behavior. Unwilling followers have to be monitored continuously; that is why dictators and despots from Stalin and Hitler to the Shah of Iran needed extensive secret police systems.

People whose job is to watch to see whether other people are doing their jobs produce nothing. Commitment diminishes the need for monitoring the behavior of people in the organization and increases the resources for productive use.

Power is limited to the people under your direct control, but your influence can pervade the entire organization. Develop your influence; it is a necessary complement to power.

You may be the leader, but you cannot give orders to everybody. To get things done you need to influence people to your point of view. Your ability to influence people is directly related to their sense of obligation to you. The web of indebtedness accomplishes more than naked power. This is the rule of reciprocation. Sociologists claim that there is no human society that does not subscribe to this rule.

If you enhance the self-image of the people in the organization, they will reciprocate by attempting to act in accordance with it.

If you make people believe in themselves, they will overcome the insurmountable and achieve the impossible. The greatest danger to totalitarianism and the strongest bulwark of democracy is the self-image of a free people.

A river starting in the mountains believes in its kinship with the ocean. It crosses all obstacles and soon is within reach of what seemed so distant at the source. An athlete who has doubts has already lost before the competition begins. The most common reason given for the success that comes from following a good leader is that "he or she made us believe we could do it."

●
37

To get things done it is important to "have friends in low places."

These friends can provide invaluable information about what is really happening throughout the organization. They are also a most valuable conduit of influence. Be good to them and they will put in the extra effort that will increase the chances for success of your plans and policies. They will convince their peers of the rightness of your actions.

Attention to the concerns of others creates obligations. Show concern for what is important to the people in your organization. They will respond with concern for what is important to you.

In a family a spouse may agree to go to the opera with the expectation that in the future the family will attend a ballgame. Attendance at children's functions creates the obligation in the children to attend certain adult events.

As a business executive you should actively participate in employee training, development, and recognition programs and show concern for providing superior health benefits. In return, the employees will help your strategies and plans succeed. Which of us has not felt special when somebody important has remembered our name and asked after our family? A successful leader makes others feel important.

Develop around you a core of people who are committed to your vision. These are the people who will move through the organization spreading and implementing the vision.

You cannot do everything yourself. The most efficient way to get things done is through a committed core group. Presidents have chiefs of staff and special assistants, CEOs have management teams, and Christ had disciples. Even the best of visions needs a core group for implementation. When you rise in the organization, make sure your replacement is loyal to you and to your vision and strategy.

Process is important to the organization. Strategy alone is not enough. If strategy represents the head, then process represents the heart of an organization.

Strategies are more likely to be successful if process considerations are included in their development. From athletics to art, your appreciation increases if you have tried to do it yourself. You can motivate best if you appreciate the challenge of the task.

Process creates results out of ideas. Many people like process. Pay attention to them — they get things done. Like fine mechanics, they pay attention to detail. They make sure that each cog in the machine is well oiled and that every breakdown is promptly repaired. Process often makes the difference between success and failure. Leaders may think strategy wins battles, but any field commander knows that battles are won in the trenches.

In business your strategy is only as good as the people who carry it out. Process-oriented employees generate profits. It is not only the grand design of the garden but also those who water and take care of it that make it beautiful.

●
39

Your personal example is the greatest influence on the organization. When you are committed and dedicated to your work, your staff will ask themselves, "Can we do less?" Even here, the reciprocity principle is at work.

The organization will do as you do. Speeches are effective only if they are consistent with your actions. As Descartes said, "It is custom and example that persuade us more than any certain knowledge." Talk all you like, but it is your personal example that permeates the organization. If good, like water it can make a desert bloom; if bad, like a cancer it will destroy.

Getting things done requires organization. Your organization should be structured to accomplish your vision. A vehicle that is haphazardly designed and constructed will not be able to get you to your destination.

Just as the design of your transportation system should be a function of the nature of the journey, the design of your organization must be consistent with your vision and the environment in which you operate. Your organization must identify positions of accountability. These are points of influence that you must control. You should place in these positions people who are committed to your vision.

You must recognize that organizational design and controls cannot account for the infinite variety of human behavior. However, the superior leader knows how to manage the human factor.

The unpredictability of human behavior can frustrate the implementation of carefully developed plans. In business, for example, understanding the techniques of marketing, finance, and manufacturing counts for little without proper implementation. And implementation depends on individuals, not theories. As Clausewitz wrote in his classic *On War:* "Each part is composed of individuals, every one of whom retains its potential of friction. . . . Friction, as we choose to call it, is a force that makes the apparently easy so difficult."

The best lubricants against organizational friction are the trust, loyalty, and commitment of the people in your organization. Promote these values. Without them, the heat generated by this friction will consume your organization.

41

"Change provides opportunity for innovation. Change gives you the chance to demonstrate your creativity."

4

CHANGE

Change is the natural order of things. Change is welcomed by the superior leader because it provides the opportunity to excel.

Change cannot be avoided. It must be accounted for in everything you do.

Change can be a result of events outside your control. Through better planning, early recognition of problems and opportunities, and quick response, you can move your organization ahead of the competition during periods of change.

As a leader you can be an agent of change. Positive leaders initiate change when they see injustice and lack of integrity. They recognize that taking advantage of the opportunity to change things for the better is the challenge of leadership.

●
43

Change provides the opportunity for innovation. It gives you the chance to demonstrate your creativity.

In the family, even commonplace occurrences like changes in mortgage rates provide opportunities for the leader, through better planning and appropriate response, to improve the family's financial position.

In business, changes in technology, regulations, and customer preferences can cause disruptions in the normal business flow. You should consider them opportunities that challenge your abilities. Executives who effectively take advantage of these opportunities can lead their companies to superior performance. You do not even have to be the first to recognize the change, just the best at effectively using the opportunity.

It is often more important to recognize the present than to predict the future.

If there are great rewards for correctly anticipating change, there are also great dangers in being wrong. Do not try to be precise about the future. If you are among the first to recognize and react to change *after it has occurred,* you will be very successful. Be precise about the present. If you do not understand the reality of your present situation, it is likely that you will be wrong about the future.

You do not have to be the first to know something to be successful. It is the effective application of knowledge that creates success.

It is not necessary to set the trend. It is more important to recognize the trend as it occurs and then act accordingly. Learn from the mistakes of those who are first, but do not let them get too far out in front. It is like auto racing: Let the front-runner break through the wall of air and make your going easier. But if you fall too far behind, the wall closes again and you have to work harder to catch up.

In the early part of the twentieth century most of the important scientific discoveries were made in Europe, but it was Americans who later applied these ideas successfully to industrial development. Since the 1970s, Japan and other Asian nations have applied fundamental technological and scientific ideas developed in the United States to achieve their own industrial success.

You have to be concerned about changes that are related to long-range trends as well as those that modify operating assumptions. A superior leader is one who is not mired in policies that are inappropriate for changed conditions.

Every leader in business, politics, or the community makes assumptions that form the basis of strategy. At regular intervals you must examine your assumptions in these areas and evaluate the consequences of various changes. When change makes the assumptions invalid, then strategy and plans have to be modified. Do not waste your efforts fighting the last war, or even the current war with obsolete weapons.

If you have thought through what you will do when certain changes occur, you will be able to react quickly once the changes take place.

You obviously cannot plan for all possible changes. It is the combination of the chance of occurrence and the magnitude of the impact that you have to consider. Events that have a high likelihood of occurrence and a potentially large impact on your activities are the ones you should concentrate on. In business, if 95% of your suppliers, manufacturing facilities, and markets are in the United States, you should not spend your time worrying about international currency exchange rates. If your business is related to oil imports, it may be prudent to develop contingency plans for various Middle East conflict scenarios.

Change does not mean that you change your principles. You should be flexible in strategy and plans but firm in principles.

Just as the most successful people change their strategies with respect to new circumstances without compromising their integrity, so should organizations.

In business it is always appropriate to provide superior customer service, stress product quality, and conduct your operation with integrity. Losing sight of the basic principles will always lead to trouble. The supple tree bends with the wind but maintains its roots firmly in the ground.

●
47

"You must learn to think about uncertainty. Uncertainty about what will happen in the future is a major challenge, but it is also the basis for optimism. Certainty about the future would make the management task trivial."

In every endeavor, you make assumptions about the future. You forecast either explicitly or implicitly. You have to guess at the future in order to make predictions.

Change is inevitable. Predicting the magnitude, direction, and timing of change is the challenge. Since you cannot know the future precisely, there is always the element of uncertainty in your assumptions and the resulting forecasts. After all, you make assumptions because you are uncertain; otherwise you would have facts.

It is your responsibility to assess the uncertainty associated with the possibility of changed conditions and other events that influence your business. You cannot be paralyzed by uncertainty; you have to make decisions. Understanding the uncertainty associated with change will help you be decisive.

You must learn to think about uncertainty. Certainty about the future would make the management task trivial. Uncertainty about what will happen in the future is a major challenge, but it is also the basis for optimism. It gives you a chance to excel.

There are procedures for quantifying uncertainty. The most common form for expressing uncertainty is in terms of odds, like the Las Vegas betting line on horse races, football games, and championship fights.

Precise quantification of uncertainty occurs in repetitive situations where large amounts of data can be collected. Life and auto insurance premiums are based on this kind of data.

Your important decisions are not repetitive; therefore you have to make judgmental estimates about uncertainty. Your experience and intuition will have to be your guide. There can be considerable difference of opinion among reasonable and knowledgeable people about the degree of uncertainty in a specific situation. There are techniques that will help you make judgments on the level of uncertainty, but there are no experts in quantifying uncertainty. All judgments, *including your own*, should be treated with skepticism.

●
49

Be careful of vague estimates of uncertainty. People can have very different ideas of what these phrases mean. This can result in serious mistakes.

It is appropriate to ask what is meant by phrases such as "there is small (great) chance"; "it is (un)likely"; "there is a probability." People have very different ideas of what phrases like these mean, and yet they often use such terms in reaching important decisions.

A well-known study that examined this issue in the legal profession surveyed approximately 350 judges to determine their understanding of what "beyond a reasonable doubt" meant. One-third of the judges thought it required that there be 100% probability that the defendant was guilty, and the other two-thirds had a variety of responses, starting at 50%. Jurors' responses also covered a wide range — a worrisome issue for a defendant.

In projections of market share, profitability, completion dates, and so on, phrases such as "we have a good chance of reaching" and "it is very likely" can have vastly different meanings, even within a small decision-making group. These differences of interpretation can lead to significant misunderstandings and unanticipated consequences.

You should try to quantify the uncertainty in probabilistic terms. It is not precision that counts but the necessity that the decision group all be speaking the same language.

Lack of quantification of probability may have led to the 1961 Bay of Pigs fiasco. A "fair chance of success," as assumed by the invasion's proponents, was interpreted by presidential advisers as being much higher than the 30% that the experts in the Pentagon had assumed in stating their opinion.

Quantification may have been one of the reasons that precluded an American air strike in the 1962 Cuban missile crisis. Air Force generals could only assure President Kennedy with a 90% probability of the effectiveness of a "surgical" air strike to eliminate the Soviet missiles in Cuba.

●
51

Ego and overconfidence can lead to great errors in judgment on estimates of uncertainty.

Even though no other project has been finished on time, you think because you are in charge something different will happen. Use comparisons with similar situations to develop your sense of the uncertainty involved. Try to identify the sources of the uncertainty. You may be able to do something about some of them. Beware of decisions made "on the average" — you can drown in a stream in which the average water depth is two feet.

All important strategic decisions are made under conditions of uncertainty. This involves risks.

Decisions made under uncertainty require you to take risks. What is risk? It is the chance that adverse consequences will occur. When there is uncertainty and you make a decision, you take a risk. You can think of risk (adverse consequences) in two ways: (a) you can be worse off than you were before the decision, or (b) you can be worse off compared with another alternative you could have chosen.

To manage the risk you may be taking you need to focus on two components: (a) the *chance* (probability) of adverse consequences, and (b) the *magnitude* of the adverse consequences.

To control risks you can reduce either the probabilities or the magnitude of adverse consequences. The probabilities are greatly influenced by the triggering event, which you may or may not be able to control. In a family context, you cannot influence inflation or predict illness-related expenses. However, by controlling expenses and increasing savings you can greatly decrease the magnitude of the impact of these external events on your family's finances.

In a business context, you cannot control natural disasters, interest rates, or potential technological change; but you can exercise some control over customer service, costs, product quality, and employee turnover and thus minimize the negative impact of external events.

If you are going to take large risks, tell your colleagues what you are doing; be sure they realize that you understand both the risks and the rewards.

We all love risk takers if they involve us in the process. If they fail, we are quick to acknowledge that the risk of failure is inherent in striving for extraordinary achievement. Mountain climbers, lone sailors going around the world, and entrepreneurs are heroes even when they fail.

If you have to make decisions when the future is very uncertain, choose a resilient course of action.

A person who follows a resilient strategy takes risks but controls the magnitude of adverse consequences. You may have to sacrifice high rewards to protect yourself from catastrophic consequences. In business, betting your company and career on events outside your control is the way of a gambler, not an executive. A wise leader always has contingency plans.

●
53

Changes in the organizational environment are inevitable. The successful leader manages these changes to his or her overall advantage.

Management changes, mergers and acquisitions, new ventures, geographic expansion, and other such activities may occur in any organization.

You must look for these changes, since they are opportunities. Accept the new challenges that are offered; seek out opportunities that fit your talents. Always look for ways to demonstrate your superior skill.

At times, changes outside your control will be unfavorable to you, to the organization, or both. But you must persevere. Circumstances will change again; you can be sure of it.

Once you grasp the inevitability of change, cooperating with it and taking advantage become easy. Just as a river negotiates changes in terrain, finding weaknesses in the rock to cut deep gorges in the mountains and developing wide meanders in the plains to reach its ultimate destination, you must change your approach with circumstances but not lose sight of your destination.

❝You, as the leader in the organization, have to act as if circumstances have changed. Your personal behavior is the major influence in convincing others to accept change. ❞

It is not easy to accept and respond to changes that modify the fundamental assumptions on which you have based your strategy.

Even exceptional individuals have difficulty accepting change. Scientists and scholars find it difficult to accept new theories; politicians and business executives find it difficult to accept new realities. Parents find it difficult to accept new relationships with their children as they become adults. Henry Ford would not acknowledge that changes in customer economic conditions and preferences had made the single-model mass-production car company obsolete. After World War II, with independence for the colonies inevitable, Winston Churchill found it difficult to accept the end of the British Empire. Many U.S. industries refuse to accept the reality of global competition and markets.

Even after changes have occurred, some people refuse to accept them. They argue that it is temporary or that there is something wrong with the data. The real reason is that they don't want to change their ways. The quicker you accept change and move on, the more positive your leadership will be.

●
55

Your acceptance of changed conditions is not enough. You also have to ensure that the organization is responsive to these changed conditions. This is a formidable task.

It is relatively easy to accept change at the intellectual level. Modifying behavior is a much more difficult task. Most leaders, whether in business, politics, or other activities, have a vested interest in leaving things as they are. All of us tend to choose the path of least resistance. This means that we tend to stick with familiar ways of doing things, even when they may be inappropriate for changed conditions. That is why, as Eric Hoffer has pointed out, it is from the ranks of those who have a small stake in the status quo that the risk takers, adventurers, explorers, and entrepreneurs arise.

You, as a leader in the organization, have to act as if circumstances have changed. Your personal behavior is the major influence in convincing others to accept change.

Action is the most powerful communicator of your acceptance of change. You cannot continue with unrestrained spending if you want everybody else to reduce expenses. Despite your exhortations, and even threats, your bureaucracy will subvert your plans. There are too many people to control without their commitment. If they see your actions as different from what you say you want them to do, they will follow your actions — not your words. They believe that the way you act is what you really want.

Strategies and operating plans must be modified to accommodate change; but this alone is not enough. Your resource allocation decisions must also reflect these changes.

People believe you when you put your energies and resources where your words are. If you think people should work harder, you must show them that you are working harder. If you say that under changed conditions R&D and marketing have become more important, then you must increase the budgets and staff in these departments. Without that, people will not believe you. If you say the business needs to automate but do not provide the funds to buy the equipment, you will not be believed. The organization will continue to do things the old way, and it will be swept away by the winds of change.

Reward those who act in accordance with changed circumstances. Your acknowledgment of appropriate behavior is a powerful motivating factor.

Organizational acceptance of changed conditions consists of the sum of individual acceptances of changed conditions. When you acknowledge appropriate behavior on the part of individuals, it encourages others to follow suit because they believe you think it is important.

Change is difficult to accept. You as a leader have to do everything you can to encourage others to accept changed circumstances.

"**You** must be able to identify, nur- ture, and control the opposites that need to coexist in your organization. A posi- tive leader sees the harmony within the diversity. "

5

PARADOX

Examine the history of business, war, politics, or any other human endeavor and you will find that enduring success requires the balance of opposing tendencies. As a leader, understanding and managing this balance will be one of your most challenging tasks.

The best athletic teams are balanced in offense and defense, individual and team play, aggression and calmness, and daring and conservatism. Overemphasis in any one area is a weakness that a competitor can exploit.

In business, government, or any other organizational activity, a leader must recognize the necessary opposites and manage them. Your organization should be like water, which has within it, in balance, all the strategies it needs. It can be a waterfall, a raging torrent, a lazily meandering stream, or a patient eroder of the hardest rock. It depends on what is needed. The existence and balance of opposites is universal.

As a positive leader you will recognize that the nurturing of opposites is necessary for progress.

In the complex endeavor of dealing with human beings, with their infinite variations, and events beyond one's control, it would be arrogant to think that there is one right way. The Right Way includes all the right ways.

It requires intellectual effort to see the need for opposites, wisdom to see the harmony in opposites, and discipline to encourage and keep alive within the organization the approach that is not dominant at the present time.

It is the wise coach who allows the gifted athlete to be unorthodox.

If you do not nurture opposites, the organization will lose its ability to adapt and be creative under new conditions.

New strategies are required to meet new challenges. To develop them you must have a diversity of views within the organization. Old assumptions have to be challenged and new realities have to be developed. People who are mired in believing that there is one right strategy for achieving success will sooner or later lead you to failure.

Without the presence of opposites, the organization will soon develop a system of decision making that simply reinforces past decisions.

You must be able to identify, nurture, and control the opposites that need to coexist in your organization. This is the principle of *controlled strategic diversity.* **The existence of opposites within the organization may puzzle others in the organization. As a positive leader, you will see the harmony within the diversity.**

The opposites that need to be nurtured in your organization are dependent on your vision and objectives and on the competitive environment. In national policy, pursuit of peace is balanced with preparedness for war; the need for energy has to be managed concurrently with the preservation of the environment; and trade-offs need to be made between providing social services and military weapons. Business requires a balance between centralization and decentralization, between long-term income and short-term profits, and between product benefits and costs.

In most of our activities, as in nature, a balance between opposites is required for success. If you want to ride a horse you have to learn to tighten and loosen the reins. In any sport, from tennis to archery, the instrument must be taut but the body relaxed. Members of the cat family, when stalking prey, remain still for long periods of time and then move with great quickness. They need these diametrically opposed skills to succeed.

The nurturing of opposites also encourages the recognition that there is no one right answer. There are many answers. This kind of approach encourages skepticism about infallibility.

●
61

Your strategic thinking will balance the attitude of "sticking to your knitting" with the search for new opportunities.

The conventional wisdom is to stick to what you know how to do. This must be balanced by adopting new strategies and skills for new conditions. Circumstances change. What you know how to do may no longer be relevant. As an individual, you may have to change careers if there is no demand for your job skills.

Your business may tend toward obsolescence and go the way of steam locomotives and whalebone corsets. You must continually evaluate your business and all its components for obsolescence. Obsolescence can come from many sources — technology, customer preferences, regulations, and competition. "Sticking to your knitting" with tunnel vision can be just as dangerous as putting your money in businesses you do not understand.

You need short-term successes without compromising your commitment to long-term goals.

Without short-term successes you will find it difficult to maintain the organization's commitment to long-term goals. The short-term successes you achieve must be on the path for reaching your vision. If you sacrifice long-term goals for short-term successes, you will not leave anything of lasting value.

As a positive leader, your control system will combine the requirement of strict adherence to plan with the ability to pursue new opportunities and respond to contingencies as they arise.

Organizational discipline is a key to achieving your objectives, but the organization must have the flexibility to react to new opportunities. This is true in family, business, and national contexts. In the family, budgets must be adhered to; but contingencies such as illnesses and opportunities such as sales also have to be managed.

In business, financial discipline is an essential component of effective management. Compliance with budgets and schedules and the control systems that monitor these activities are keys to profitability. To pursue new opportunities may require deviation from the budget. Sticking to the plan may result in loss of market share and strategic positioning for the future. It is your job as a leader to create an environment where the control systems balance adherence to the plan with initiative.

In planning for the future you will include incremental ideas that fit easily into the current system and innovative ideas that require restructuring the organization.

In national policy, both new legislation and amendments to improve existing laws help meet new problems. In foreign policy, support for existing governments has to be balanced with support for revolutionary forces that are attempting to overthrow what we perceive as unjust systems.

In business, the easiest products and services to develop and introduce are "incremental" products, ones that require minimal adjustment on the part of the organization and the customer. "New and improved" toothpastes, soaps, and detergents are examples. These are necessary for protecting market share and increasing profits.

You must also develop innovative products; otherwise you can be outflanked and your product line made obsolete. Being the first to introduce new products and services allows you to set the price and establish a dominant market share, resulting in superior levels of profitability.

You must balance the risks and long-term view of innovation with the short-term view and conservatism of incrementalism.

Efficient implementation requires centralized decision making, but you, as a positive leader, will also encourage entrepreneurial behavior by providing decision-making autonomy at operational levels.

In any organization, including the family, the leaders (the parents) have to balance the need for individuals (the children) to make independent decisions with the need for centralized decisions for the long-range common good.

There has to be centralized control, but managers in the field have to be allowed to make decisions to take advantage of opportunities that result from changed conditions. If you allow centralized decision making to stifle operational-level decisions, you will lose your best managers and sink into mediocrity.

Centralized decision making breeds bureaucracy, creates bottlenecks, and makes preservation of power a dominant objective.

Entrepreneurial managers require financial commitment from the leaders. They are optimists who believe that success is always just around the corner.

In business you must balance the need for control with the potential for bureaucratic paralysis and the need to support entrepreneurial managers with the danger of pouring money into a bottomless pit.

●
65

As a positive leader you will support the development of consensus by adequate committee work while avoiding the paralysis that comes from trying to accommodate everyone.

Effective implementation requires the building of consensus. Different viewpoints need to be considered. Committees and staff work are necessary. Strong action-oriented leaders do not have the patience for committee work, and yet, you cannot manage complex organizations without committees. It is a negative leader who denigrates committees by saying that "a camel is a horse designed by a committee." Obviously, he or she never had to choose between a horse and a camel to cross a desert.

Committees provide the checks and balances for strong-willed leaders who, left to their own devices, may plunge into waters too deep.

Committees can also result in nonaction — decisions may not get made because there are too many people to convince. You must, therefore, learn when to take command. You cannot delegate all responsibility to a committee if you wish to get things done.

You need to encourage generalists who have the ability to integrate across disciplines and specialists who can give expert opinions in narrow areas.

As issues get more complicated, expert opinion is essential to making good decisions. The management of national affairs requires experts in defense, foreign affairs, economics, health services, and education to develop successful policy. In business, specialists in finance, marketing, information systems, and other areas are essential to success.

However, decisions involve the interaction of these specialty areas. At the decision points the organization needs generalists who have the ability to integrate across specialty areas. A specialty is often required before one can be a generalist; it is the discipline of developing a specialty that is valuable. The person with depth in one area and breadth across many has the right background to be a generalist.

●
67

You have to balance and nurture the legitimate competing interests of the various constituencies in your organization.

It is necessary to balance and nurture the aspirations of siblings in a family while balancing the family unit's goals. The same axiom can be applied to the legitimate goals of different interest groups at the national level.

In business, shareholders' interests are important because it is the shareholders who provide the capital. Can you have less concern for employees who give of themselves?

In your dealings with members of the organization and the public at large, pay attention to both form and substance.

Substance is important, and so is image. Both are essential to leadership. Perception is crucial. The organization must be perceived as a leader by its customers and its employees, and those in charge must be perceived as leaders within the organization. People do not have the time to analyze and reflect and make judgments based solely on substance. They use shortcuts; impressions and image are the data for the shortcuts.

Do not be deluded that cream always rises to the top. There are imitation products, and many people cannot tell the difference.

"You need short-term successes without compromising long-term goals."

A leader must balance the twin motivational forces of self-sacrifice and self-interest. Self-sacrifice is inspired by the vision for the organization and self-interest by the desire to advance within the organization.

The conflict between self-interest and self-sacrifice is present in all of us. As Rabbi Hillel asked, "If I am not for myself, then who is for me? And if I am not for others, then who am I?"

The leader who has a great cause asks for sacrifices and does not need to offer rewards. Churchill offered the British people "blood, sweat, and tears" when he inspired them to their "finest hour." In an organizational setting, self-interest is also an important factor in motivating people. A positive leader, recognizing this, motivates by appealing to the positive concepts of advancement through cooperation, fairness, and integrity. The CEO who relies on incentive compensation as the major motivating force fosters destructive competition among people in the organization, encourages success at any price, and is likely to have no vision for the business.

●
69

An organization that becomes extreme in its commitment to any specific criteria for judging performance will lack flexibility. It will be unable to respond to changed conditions.

Empires that concentrated on their armies were destroyed not by outside forces but by internal dissension. They had a one-dimensional view of national policy — conquest — and neglected the needs of their people. Similarly, individuals who evaluate their achievements only on the basis of money will have difficulty maintaining the emotional relationships in a family.

If you run your business on the single criterion of yearly profitability, you will not invest in R&D or new technologies and equipment. One-dimensional organizations succeed only in very specific circumstances for a limited period of time.

You must always make sure that the organization has people who are experienced with alternative approaches to strategic and operational problems. Nurture them in small business areas within the organization.

You must demonstrate that you have an open mind for competing approaches. Management strategies and operating procedures have to be learned by doing. You must allow a level of experimentation in parts of your business. This is necessary for people to expend the energy to develop innovative ideas in support of strategies that may be currently out of favor.

As a positive leader, you must be able to see the forest *and* the individual trees.

You have to be able to both see the big picture and pay attention to details. If you devote your attention to either one exclusively, you court failure. To fully appreciate a painting you must be able to see both the composition and the brushwork.

Not paying attention to detail can cause embarrassment and lead people to think you are not in control — Ronald Reagan's perceived problem. If you do not emphasize your grasp of the "big picture" and concentrate on details, you will be perceived as lacking direction — Jimmy Carter's perceived problem.

Nurturing opposites does not mean parity. It is up to you to decide which of the opposites should predominate at any one time. Nurturing opposites must be controlled. It does not mean lack of discipline; in fact, it requires great discipline.

Do not confuse keeping an open mind and encouraging opposites with lack of focus and indecision. It is still necessary to select a course of action and keep your organization committed to it. Commitment to a course of action while encouraging independent thinking is a challenge of leadership.

"Manage your-self. This is the most important activity of a leader.**"**

6

CHARACTER

As a leader you are a person of action. Actions without values are dangerous, and values without action are impotent. The values embodied in your actions are the manifestation of your character.

The quality of your leadership is founded in your character. Professional competence is necessary but is not sufficient for leadership. It is your "active ethical value system" —the values you live by—that will determine your success as a leader. Your personal qualities of courage and determination will enable you to act in accordance with your values. As a positive leader, your actions will always be based on the values of truth and justice.

Success and failure in an organization are determined by the character of the leaders. The decline of Rome did not begin because its armies were weak; the decline started when the leaders succumbed to the arrogance of power and forsook honor and justice.

Manage yourself. The development of character is an exercise in self-management. This is the most important activity of a leader.

Self-management is totally under your control, but the results of managing others are always unpredictable. The values and qualities of a positive leader are present in all of us. Ordinary people, through self-evaluation and self-discipline, can become extraordinary leaders. From the Greeks at Thermopylae to the marchers at Selma, a group of ordinary individuals performed heroic deeds because of an active ethical value system.

Development of an active ethical value system is not an intellectual exercise. It is your commitment to yourself. You may make mistakes in the application of your value system when you do not understand a specific situation. Positive leaders do not always have to be right, but they must always be trying to do the right thing. Admit your mistakes. Do not be afraid to ask others in the organization for help. When your value system is above reproach, your leadership position will endure.

You will always act according to your active ethical value system. Purpose and process will be equally important—there will be a fusion of ends and means.

Positive leadership is not limited to the narrow objective of winning as defined by short-term success. Winning at any price is not acceptable to a positive leader. Your short-term successes will always be founded in an active ethical value system. Such successes are the building blocks of that lasting achievement which is beyond winning.

You are not discouraged when you see individuals and organizations that have gained power and riches through fear, intimidation, and questionable practices. You know that these short-term successes will not endure and that there is a cost that may not be readily visible. There is always a price to pay for unethical actions, just as in economics "there are no free lunches." Even nations that built their prosperity on unethical actions have always had to pay a price.

Because your value system is based on justice, you are motivated by cooperation for achievement, not competition to gain power.

An organization motivated by justice and the desire for lasting achievement will always, over the long term, outperform an organization motivated solely by material gain. In the life cycle of a family, business, or nation there is always a time when material benefits decline. Unemployment, recession, or a natural calamity can have profound effects. But when the people are confident of being treated with justice, they will remain dedicated and committed to the organization. They will make sacrifices and adapt to change; innovation will flourish and the organization will reach higher levels of achievement.

There is no justice when executives take large bonuses and lay off workers. There can be no appeal to dedication, commitment, sacrifice and partnership. In such businesses, management and workers are in competition. They do not cooperate for the benefit of the organization. When everybody is interested only in short-term gain, there is no investment in the future.

By your personal example you will inspire a commitment to integrity throughout the organization. Organizations committed to integrity are successful and will endure.

Your integrity requires you to accept the responsibility for the mistakes and failures of the organization. The leader who passes the burden of failure to others in the organization is not a positive leader. Leaders who disavow explicit instructions, selectively remember approvals for actions, and hide behind technicalities to escape responsibility create a climate of distrust and fear. They stifle the productivity of their organization and limit performance.

Your intellectual honesty will compel you to use ideas generated by others and always give credit. Your integrity does not allow you to select only those facts that support a preconceived position. Therefore, creativity and openness flourish under your leadership and the organization under your leadership will remain innovative.

A business committed to integrity does not compromise on safety or quality. Such companies have superior long-term financial performance.

●
77

The character of your advisers and staff will have a significant influence on the quality of your leadership. Select such people with great care, since the master is judged by the pupils.

The cabinets and staff of presidents, advisers to monarchs, and the management teams of corporate chief executives have often determined the success of their leaders. When you attain leadership, many will wish to share your power. They will say what they think you want to hear. Evaluate people on the basis of actions, not words. Judge people in high places by how they act on little things and people in low places by their stand on important issues. Individuals of courage and integrity cannot be "yes men"; commitment to their value system will not permit it. Select your advisers from among this group. As a positive leader you will have the wisdom to nurture such people and value their opinions.

❝ It is your "active ethical value system"—the values you live by—that will determine your success as a leader. ❞

Your value system must be evident to all. People must be able to rely on it. Acting according to your value system creates trust. A positive leader is a trusted leader.

In everything you do—speeches, writings, and above all, actions—you must maintain your commitment to your value system. As a leader you will find many opportunities for gaining advantage by not telling the truth, by being vindictive in the exercise of power, and by being arrogant in the belief that you are always right. Many around you will encourage this kind of behavior, but the measure of your positive leadership is how well you resist these temptations.

The value systems of leaders permeate their organizations. Value systems that appeal to justice and benevolence create organizations that are forces for great positive change.

When people in an organization can trust their leaders, they devote themselves to attaining the objectives of the organization. They work hard because they are confident that every attempt will be made to treat them fairly. A belief in justice is the most powerful motivator for hard work. It is the basis for the long-term economic success of democracy. Superior financial performance based on higher levels of productivity always comes from employees who believe that their leaders are committed to a system of just rewards.

Courage and will are the dominant personality qualities in a positive leader. Without them you cannot maintain your commitment when the going gets rough.

Without will and determination you may give up too early, but without courage you will never get started. Courage does not mean that you do not accept the possibility of failure. You recognize the possibility and are still willing to go forward, confident in your determination to overcome the obstacles that are likely to arise.

With courage you will dare to take risks, have the strength to be compassionate and the wisdom to be humble. Courage is essential for integrity. The challenge to your integrity comes when you have the power to make the rules and when you have to go against the currents of acceptable behavior. You will need courage to maintain your commitment to your values.

To succeed, you must be determined and have the will to overcome obstacles.

People want to see in their leaders the will and determination to reach the goals that have been set. From family leaders to CEOs, the projection of an indomitable will is a source of inspiration.

You must have the will to survive when circumstances are unfavorable, to persevere when your ideas are not accepted, and to continue when the results of your initial efforts are not encouraging.

"I will overcome" is the creed of everybody who has reached the top.

Leadership is a performing art. You have to practice in order to excel. It is not merely a technique; leadership is a way of life.

You have all the qualities of a leader. When the opportunity presents itself, you can climb to the summit of positive leadership. It is in your hands. But intellectual brilliance alone will not make you a positive leader. The essential requirements are an active ethical value system, courage, and will.

In everything you do, whether you are seeking short-term results or striving for long-term goals, you act according to your ethical value system.

Your success endures because your example inspires others to develop an ethical value system and have the courage and will to consistently act according to those values.

●
81

❝With courage you will dare to take risks, have the strength to be compassionate and the wisdom to be humble. Courage is the foundation of integrity. ❞

"The wheel of leadership is before you. The hub is your character. The spokes of action, power, influence, change, and paradox derive strength from your character and keep the wheel moving."

EPILOGUE

The symbolic fast for forty days and nights in the desert was a preparation for leadership. If you want to be a leader, you must similarly prepare yourself.

- Be courageous and compassionate.
- Develop self-discipline and determination.
- Be willing to influence, decide, and act, but always with integrity.
- Gain knowledge and insight.
- Face the moral dilemmas that come with power.

The wheel of leadership is before you. The hub is your character. The spokes of action, power, influence, change, and paradox derive strength from your character and keep the wheel moving.

Being an effective leader can help causes and people. Your leadership will be measured by the achievements of your organization and the people in it. If you have been successful, not only will the organization have achieved the vision you set before it, some of the people you have led will have developed the qualities to become leaders in their own right. As the Chinese philosopher Lao-tzu observed, the greatest leader is one about whom, after he leaves, the people say, "We did these things ourselves."

Everybody has an opportunity to exercise leadership — in politics, business, community activities, and many other organizational contexts, including the family. That leadership should be guided by thought grounded in your character.

Leadership implies responsibility to others. Positive leaders are driven by their vision and not by a quest for power. They rise to the top on the shoulders of the people who believe in their leadership. They retain their integrity even in changing circumstances. When leadership is the gift of those who are led, it exists in its most exalted form. When the people in your organization feel that they are fortunate to have you as their leader, you have the resources to achieve greatness.

ABOUT THE AUTHOR

Dr. Keshavan Nair has over 25 years experience in business management, teaching, and consulting in the United States, Europe, the Middle East, and the Far East. He has published extensively in technical and management journals. His next book provides additional insight into leadership in action, based on a study of the lives of Gandhi and Genghis Khan. With an educational and cultural background developed in Eastern and Western environments, he is also interested in philosophy, history, and religion. Dr. Nair provides business and management consulting services through Benjamin/Nair, Inc., with offices in San Francisco, California, and Phoenix, Arizona.